50 Mastering Miso Recipes

By: Kelly Johnson

Table of Contents

- Spicy Miso Noodles
- Miso-Maple Glazed Roasted Carrots
- Miso-Butter Corn
- Miso Sweet Potato Mash
- Miso and Sesame Cucumber Salad
- Miso-Infused Risotto
- Miso-Scallion Pancakes
- Miso and Peanut Butter Dip
- Miso-Marinated Beef Skewers
- Miso-Braised Pork Belly
- Miso-Roasted Mushrooms
- Miso-Avocado Toast
- Miso and Green Bean Salad
- Miso-Infused Pesto
- Miso and Shitake Mushroom Soup
- Miso-Maple Roasted Squash
- Miso Braised Short Ribs
- Miso and Soba Noodle Salad
- Miso and Coconut Soup
- Miso-Glazed Tofu Bites
- Miso and Garlic Sautéed Greens
- Miso-Marinated Tempeh
- Miso-Mustard Grilled Chicken
- Miso and Lemon Grilled Shrimp
- Miso Braised Duck
- Miso-Infused Creamy Polenta
- Miso and Lime Shrimp Tacos
- Spicy Miso Dressing for Salads
- Miso-Infused Vegetable Tempura
- Miso Pork Ramen
- Miso-Curry Rice
- Miso Gravy for Mashed Potatoes
- Miso and Pumpkin Soup
- Miso-Cilantro Rice
- Miso-Lime Chicken Skewers

- Miso and Chive Dip
- Miso Soba Noodle Soup
- Miso-Marinated Roasted Chicken
- Miso and Lemon Cod
- Miso Cabbage Rolls
- Miso-Fennel Soup
- Miso-Cucumber Sushi Rolls

Spicy Miso Noodles

Ingredients:

- 4 oz noodles (soba, ramen, or udon)
- 2 tbsp white miso paste
- 1 tbsp sesame oil
- 1 tbsp soy sauce
- 1 tbsp rice vinegar
- 1 tsp chili paste (or to taste)
- 1 tbsp honey
- 2 cloves garlic, minced
- 1/2 cup green onions, chopped

Instructions:

1. **Cook the Noodles**: Boil the noodles according to the package instructions, then drain and set aside.
2. **Prepare the Sauce**: In a bowl, whisk together miso paste, sesame oil, soy sauce, rice vinegar, chili paste, honey, and garlic.
3. **Combine**: Toss the cooked noodles with the miso sauce until evenly coated.
4. **Serve**: Garnish with chopped green onions and serve hot.

Miso-Maple Glazed Roasted Carrots

Ingredients:

- 1 lb carrots, peeled and cut into sticks
- 2 tbsp white miso paste
- 1 tbsp maple syrup
- 1 tbsp olive oil
- 1 tbsp rice vinegar
- Salt and pepper to taste
  Instructions:

1. **Prepare the Carrots**: Preheat the oven to 400°F (200°C). Toss the carrot sticks with olive oil, salt, and pepper, and spread them on a baking sheet.
2. **Make the Glaze**: In a bowl, whisk together miso paste, maple syrup, and rice vinegar until smooth.
3. **Roast the Carrots**: Roast the carrots in the oven for 20-25 minutes, tossing halfway through.
4. **Glaze the Carrots**: Drizzle the miso-maple glaze over the roasted carrots and toss to coat evenly.
5. **Serve**: Serve hot as a side dish.

Miso-Butter Corn

Ingredients:

- 4 ears of corn, husked
- 2 tbsp unsalted butter
- 1 tbsp white miso paste
- 1 tsp soy sauce
- 1/2 tsp chili flakes (optional)
- 1/2 tsp garlic powder

Instructions:

1. **Grill the Corn**: Preheat the grill or grill pan. Grill the corn for 10-12 minutes, turning occasionally until charred and tender.
2. **Prepare the Miso-Butter**: In a small pan, melt the butter and whisk in the miso paste, soy sauce, chili flakes, and garlic powder.
3. **Coat the Corn**: Brush the miso-butter mixture over the grilled corn.
4. **Serve**: Serve immediately as a delicious side dish.

Miso Sweet Potato Mash

Ingredients:

- 2 large sweet potatoes, peeled and cubed
- 2 tbsp white miso paste
- 1 tbsp olive oil
- 1/4 cup vegetable broth
- 1/4 cup coconut milk (or regular milk)
- Salt and pepper to taste

Instructions:

1. **Boil the Sweet Potatoes**: Cook the sweet potato cubes in boiling water for 10-12 minutes until tender. Drain and return to the pot.
2. **Mash**: Mash the sweet potatoes using a potato masher or a fork.
3. **Prepare the Miso Mixture**: In a small pan, heat the olive oil and whisk in miso paste, vegetable broth, and coconut milk until smooth.
4. **Combine**: Stir the miso mixture into the mashed sweet potatoes and season with salt and pepper.
5. **Serve**: Serve hot as a savory and creamy side dish.

Miso and Sesame Cucumber Salad

Ingredients:

- 2 cucumbers, thinly sliced
- 1 tbsp white miso paste
- 1 tbsp sesame oil
- 1 tbsp rice vinegar
- 1 tsp honey
- 1 tbsp sesame seeds
- 1/4 cup green onions, chopped
- 1/2 tsp chili flakes (optional)

Instructions:

1. **Prepare the Cucumber**: Thinly slice the cucumbers and place them in a bowl.
2. **Make the Dressing**: In a small bowl, whisk together miso paste, sesame oil, rice vinegar, honey, sesame seeds, green onions, and chili flakes.
3. **Toss the Salad**: Pour the dressing over the cucumber slices and toss to combine.
4. **Serve**: Let sit for 10 minutes before serving for the flavors to meld.

Miso-Infused Risotto

Ingredients:

- 1 cup Arborio rice
- 4 cups vegetable broth
- 2 tbsp white miso paste
- 1/4 cup white wine
- 1 tbsp olive oil
- 1 small onion, chopped
- 2 cloves garlic, minced
- 1/2 cup grated Parmesan cheese
- Salt and pepper to taste

Instructions:

1. **Prepare the Miso Broth**: In a saucepan, heat the vegetable broth and whisk in the miso paste until dissolved.
2. **Cook the Risotto**: In a separate pan, heat olive oil over medium heat and sauté the onion and garlic until softened. Add the Arborio rice and cook for 1-2 minutes.
3. **Add the Wine**: Pour in the white wine and stir until absorbed.
4. **Add the Broth**: Slowly add the miso-infused broth, one ladle at a time, stirring constantly until the liquid is absorbed before adding more.
5. **Finish**: When the rice is creamy and tender, stir in Parmesan cheese and season with salt and pepper.
6. **Serve**: Serve warm as a rich and savory main or side dish.

Miso-Scallion Pancakes

Ingredients:

- 1 cup all-purpose flour
- 1/2 tsp baking powder
- 1/2 tsp white miso paste
- 1/2 cup water
- 1/4 cup chopped scallions
- 1 tbsp sesame oil
- 1 tbsp soy sauce (for dipping)
- 1/2 tsp chili paste (optional)

Instructions:

1. **Make the Batter**: In a bowl, combine flour, baking powder, miso paste, and water to make a smooth batter. Stir in chopped scallions.
2. **Cook the Pancakes**: Heat sesame oil in a pan over medium heat. Pour in small amounts of batter to form pancakes, cooking for 2-3 minutes per side until golden and crisp.
3. **Serve**: Serve with soy sauce and chili paste for dipping.

Miso and Peanut Butter Dip

Ingredients:

- 2 tbsp white miso paste
- 3 tbsp peanut butter
- 1 tbsp rice vinegar
- 1 tbsp soy sauce
- 1 tsp honey
- 1 tbsp sesame oil
- 1/2 tsp chili flakes (optional)

Instructions:

1. **Mix the Ingredients**: In a bowl, whisk together miso paste, peanut butter, rice vinegar, soy sauce, honey, sesame oil, and chili flakes until smooth.
2. **Serve**: Serve as a dip with fresh veggies, crackers, or pita bread for a savory and creamy snack or appetizer.

Miso-Marinated Beef Skewers

Ingredients:

- 1 lb beef sirloin or flank steak, cut into cubes
- 3 tbsp white miso paste
- 2 tbsp soy sauce
- 1 tbsp sesame oil
- 2 tbsp honey
- 1 tbsp rice vinegar
- 1 tsp grated ginger
- 2 cloves garlic, minced
- 1 tbsp sesame seeds (optional)

Instructions:

1. **Prepare the Marinade**: In a bowl, whisk together miso paste, soy sauce, sesame oil, honey, rice vinegar, ginger, and garlic.
2. **Marinate the Beef**: Place the beef cubes in a resealable plastic bag or bowl, pour the marinade over, and refrigerate for at least 2 hours or overnight for maximum flavor.
3. **Skewer the Beef**: Thread the marinated beef onto skewers.
4. **Grill**: Preheat a grill or grill pan over medium-high heat. Grill the skewers for 3-4 minutes on each side until cooked to your preferred level of doneness.
5. **Serve**: Garnish with sesame seeds and serve hot.

Miso-Braised Pork Belly

Ingredients:

- 1 lb pork belly, cut into 1-inch cubes
- 3 tbsp white miso paste
- 2 tbsp soy sauce
- 1 tbsp rice vinegar
- 1 tbsp sugar
- 2 cups chicken broth
- 2 cloves garlic, minced
- 1-inch piece of ginger, sliced
- 2 tbsp sesame oil

Instructions:

1. **Sear the Pork Belly**: Heat sesame oil in a large pot over medium-high heat. Brown the pork belly cubes on all sides, then remove and set aside.
2. **Prepare the Braise**: In the same pot, add the garlic, ginger, miso paste, soy sauce, rice vinegar, sugar, and chicken broth. Stir to combine and bring to a simmer.
3. **Braise the Pork Belly**: Return the pork belly to the pot, cover, and simmer on low heat for 1.5 to 2 hours, stirring occasionally, until the pork is tender.
4. **Serve**: Serve the braised pork belly with steamed rice or vegetables.

Miso-Roasted Mushrooms

Ingredients:

- 2 cups mixed mushrooms (shiitake, cremini, or button), sliced
- 2 tbsp white miso paste
- 1 tbsp olive oil
- 1 tbsp soy sauce
- 1 tsp rice vinegar
- 1/2 tsp sesame oil
- 2 cloves garlic, minced
- 1 tbsp fresh parsley, chopped

Instructions:

1. **Preheat the Oven**: Preheat your oven to 400°F (200°C).
2. **Prepare the Mushrooms**: In a large bowl, combine the mushrooms with miso paste, olive oil, soy sauce, rice vinegar, sesame oil, and garlic. Toss to coat.
3. **Roast the Mushrooms**: Spread the mushrooms on a baking sheet in a single layer. Roast for 20-25 minutes, stirring halfway through, until tender and golden.
4. **Serve**: Garnish with fresh parsley and serve as a side dish or topping for rice or noodles.

Miso-Avocado Toast

Ingredients:

- 1 ripe avocado
- 1 tbsp white miso paste
- 2 slices of toasted bread
- 1 tbsp sesame oil
- 1 tsp lemon juice
- 1/2 tsp chili flakes (optional)
- Sesame seeds for garnish

Instructions:

1. **Mash the Avocado**: In a bowl, mash the avocado with miso paste, sesame oil, lemon juice, and chili flakes.
2. **Prepare the Toast**: Spread the miso-avocado mixture on top of toasted bread.
3. **Garnish**: Sprinkle sesame seeds on top and serve immediately as a savory breakfast or snack.

Miso and Green Bean Salad

Ingredients:

- 2 cups green beans, trimmed
- 2 tbsp white miso paste
- 1 tbsp sesame oil
- 1 tbsp rice vinegar
- 1 tsp soy sauce
- 1 tsp honey
- 1/4 cup toasted sesame seeds
- 1/4 cup chopped green onions

Instructions:

1. **Blanch the Green Beans**: Bring a pot of salted water to a boil. Add the green beans and cook for 3-4 minutes until tender-crisp. Drain and immediately transfer to a bowl of ice water to stop the cooking process.
2. **Prepare the Dressing**: In a small bowl, whisk together miso paste, sesame oil, rice vinegar, soy sauce, and honey.
3. **Toss the Salad**: Toss the blanched green beans with the dressing until evenly coated.
4. **Serve**: Garnish with sesame seeds and chopped green onions. Serve chilled or at room temperature.

Miso-Infused Pesto

Ingredients:

- 1 cup fresh basil leaves
- 1/4 cup pine nuts
- 2 tbsp white miso paste
- 1/2 cup olive oil
- 2 cloves garlic
- 1/4 cup grated Parmesan cheese
    Instructions:
1. **Blend the Ingredients**: In a food processor, combine basil, pine nuts, miso paste, garlic, and Parmesan cheese.
2. **Add the Olive Oil**: While the processor is running, slowly drizzle in the olive oil until the pesto reaches your desired consistency.
3. **Serve**: Use the pesto with pasta, roasted vegetables, or as a spread.

Miso and Shiitake Mushroom Soup

Ingredients:

- 1 cup dried shiitake mushrooms
- 4 cups vegetable broth
- 2 tbsp white miso paste
- 1 tbsp soy sauce
- 1/2 tsp sesame oil
- 2 green onions, chopped
- 1 block tofu, cubed (optional)

Instructions:

1. **Rehydrate the Mushrooms**: Place the dried shiitake mushrooms in hot water for 20 minutes to rehydrate, then slice thinly.
2. **Make the Soup Base**: In a pot, combine the vegetable broth, miso paste, soy sauce, and sesame oil. Bring to a simmer.
3. **Add the Mushrooms and Tofu**: Add the sliced mushrooms and tofu (if using) to the broth. Simmer for 5-10 minutes.
4. **Serve**: Garnish with chopped green onions and serve hot.

Miso-Maple Roasted Squash

Ingredients:

- 1 medium squash (butternut or acorn), peeled and cubed
- 2 tbsp white miso paste
- 1 tbsp maple syrup
- 1 tbsp olive oil
- 1 tbsp soy sauce
- 1/2 tsp ground cinnamon

Instructions:

1. **Preheat the Oven**: Preheat your oven to 375°F (190°C).
2. **Prepare the Squash**: In a bowl, toss the cubed squash with miso paste, maple syrup, olive oil, soy sauce, and cinnamon.
3. **Roast the Squash**: Spread the squash in a single layer on a baking sheet. Roast for 25-30 minutes, flipping halfway through, until tender and golden.
4. **Serve**: Serve as a side dish or over quinoa for a hearty meal.

Miso Braised Short Ribs

Ingredients:

- 2 lbs beef short ribs
- 3 tbsp white miso paste
- 2 tbsp soy sauce
- 1 tbsp sesame oil
- 1 tbsp rice vinegar
- 3 cups beef broth
- 1-inch piece of ginger, sliced
- 2 cloves garlic, minced

Instructions:

1. **Brown the Short Ribs**: In a large pot, heat sesame oil over medium-high heat. Brown the short ribs on all sides, then remove and set aside.
2. **Prepare the Braise**: In the same pot, add the garlic, ginger, miso paste, soy sauce, rice vinegar, and beef broth. Stir to combine and bring to a simmer.
3. **Braise the Short Ribs**: Return the short ribs to the pot, cover, and simmer for 2-3 hours, until the meat is tender and falls off the bone.
4. **Serve**: Serve the braised short ribs with the braising liquid and mashed potatoes or rice.

Spicy Miso Noodles

Ingredients:

- 4 oz noodles (soba, ramen, or udon)
- 2 tbsp white miso paste
- 1 tbsp sesame oil
- 1 tbsp soy sauce
- 1 tbsp rice vinegar
- 1 tsp chili paste (or to taste)
- 1 tbsp honey
- 2 cloves garlic, minced
- 1/2 cup green onions, chopped

Instructions:

1. **Cook the Noodles**: Boil the noodles according to the package instructions, then drain and set aside.
2. **Prepare the Sauce**: In a bowl, whisk together miso paste, sesame oil, soy sauce, rice vinegar, chili paste, honey, and garlic.
3. **Combine**: Toss the cooked noodles with the miso sauce until evenly coated.
4. **Serve**: Garnish with chopped green onions and serve hot.

Miso-Maple Glazed Roasted Carrots

Ingredients:

- 1 lb carrots, peeled and cut into sticks
- 2 tbsp white miso paste
- 1 tbsp maple syrup
- 1 tbsp olive oil
- 1 tbsp rice vinegar
- Salt and pepper to taste

Instructions:

1. **Prepare the Carrots**: Preheat the oven to 400°F (200°C). Toss the carrot sticks with olive oil, salt, and pepper, and spread them on a baking sheet.
2. **Make the Glaze**: In a bowl, whisk together miso paste, maple syrup, and rice vinegar until smooth.
3. **Roast the Carrots**: Roast the carrots in the oven for 20-25 minutes, tossing halfway through.
4. **Glaze the Carrots**: Drizzle the miso-maple glaze over the roasted carrots and toss to coat evenly.
5. **Serve**: Serve hot as a side dish.

Miso-Butter Corn

Ingredients:

- 4 ears of corn, husked
- 2 tbsp unsalted butter
- 1 tbsp white miso paste
- 1 tsp soy sauce
- 1/2 tsp chili flakes (optional)
- 1/2 tsp garlic powder

Instructions:

1. **Grill the Corn**: Preheat the grill or grill pan. Grill the corn for 10-12 minutes, turning occasionally until charred and tender.
2. **Prepare the Miso-Butter**: In a small pan, melt the butter and whisk in the miso paste, soy sauce, chili flakes, and garlic powder.
3. **Coat the Corn**: Brush the miso-butter mixture over the grilled corn.
4. **Serve**: Serve immediately as a delicious side dish.

Miso Sweet Potato Mash

Ingredients:

- 2 large sweet potatoes, peeled and cubed
- 2 tbsp white miso paste
- 1 tbsp olive oil
- 1/4 cup vegetable broth
- 1/4 cup coconut milk (or regular milk)
- Salt and pepper to taste

Instructions:

1. **Boil the Sweet Potatoes**: Cook the sweet potato cubes in boiling water for 10-12 minutes until tender. Drain and return to the pot.
2. **Mash**: Mash the sweet potatoes using a potato masher or a fork.
3. **Prepare the Miso Mixture**: In a small pan, heat the olive oil and whisk in miso paste, vegetable broth, and coconut milk until smooth.
4. **Combine**: Stir the miso mixture into the mashed sweet potatoes and season with salt and pepper.
5. **Serve**: Serve hot as a savory and creamy side dish.

Miso and Sesame Cucumber Salad

Ingredients:

- 2 cucumbers, thinly sliced
- 1 tbsp white miso paste
- 1 tbsp sesame oil
- 1 tbsp rice vinegar
- 1 tsp honey
- 1 tbsp sesame seeds
- 1/4 cup green onions, chopped
- 1/2 tsp chili flakes (optional)

Instructions:

1. **Prepare the Cucumber**: Thinly slice the cucumbers and place them in a bowl.
2. **Make the Dressing**: In a small bowl, whisk together miso paste, sesame oil, rice vinegar, honey, sesame seeds, green onions, and chili flakes.
3. **Toss the Salad**: Pour the dressing over the cucumber slices and toss to combine.
4. **Serve**: Let sit for 10 minutes before serving for the flavors to meld.

Miso-Infused Risotto

Ingredients:

- 1 cup Arborio rice
- 4 cups vegetable broth
- 2 tbsp white miso paste
- 1/4 cup white wine
- 1 tbsp olive oil
- 1 small onion, chopped
- 2 cloves garlic, minced
- 1/2 cup grated Parmesan cheese
- Salt and pepper to taste

Instructions:

1. **Prepare the Miso Broth**: In a saucepan, heat the vegetable broth and whisk in the miso paste until dissolved.
2. **Cook the Risotto**: In a separate pan, heat olive oil over medium heat and sauté the onion and garlic until softened. Add the Arborio rice and cook for 1-2 minutes.
3. **Add the Wine**: Pour in the white wine and stir until absorbed.
4. **Add the Broth**: Slowly add the miso-infused broth, one ladle at a time, stirring constantly until the liquid is absorbed before adding more.
5. **Finish**: When the rice is creamy and tender, stir in Parmesan cheese and season with salt and pepper.
6. **Serve**: Serve warm as a rich and savory main or side dish.

Miso-Scallion Pancakes

Ingredients:

- 1 cup all-purpose flour
- 1/2 tsp baking powder
- 1/2 tsp white miso paste
- 1/2 cup water
- 1/4 cup chopped scallions
- 1 tbsp sesame oil
- 1 tbsp soy sauce (for dipping)
- 1/2 tsp chili paste (optional)

Instructions:

1. **Make the Batter**: In a bowl, combine flour, baking powder, miso paste, and water to make a smooth batter. Stir in chopped scallions.
2. **Cook the Pancakes**: Heat sesame oil in a pan over medium heat. Pour in small amounts of batter to form pancakes, cooking for 2-3 minutes per side until golden and crisp.
3. **Serve**: Serve with soy sauce and chili paste for dipping.

Miso and Peanut Butter Dip

Ingredients:

- 2 tbsp white miso paste
- 3 tbsp peanut butter
- 1 tbsp rice vinegar
- 1 tbsp soy sauce
- 1 tsp honey
- 1 tbsp sesame oil
- 1/2 tsp chili flakes (optional)

Instructions:

1. **Mix the Ingredients**: In a bowl, whisk together miso paste, peanut butter, rice vinegar, soy sauce, honey, sesame oil, and chili flakes until smooth.
2. **Serve**: Serve as a dip with fresh veggies, crackers, or pita bread for a savory and creamy snack or appetizer.

Miso-Marinated Beef Skewers

Ingredients:

- 1 lb beef sirloin or flank steak, cut into cubes
- 3 tbsp white miso paste
- 2 tbsp soy sauce
- 1 tbsp sesame oil
- 2 tbsp honey
- 1 tbsp rice vinegar
- 1 tsp grated ginger
- 2 cloves garlic, minced
- 1 tbsp sesame seeds (optional)

Instructions:

1. **Prepare the Marinade**: In a bowl, whisk together miso paste, soy sauce, sesame oil, honey, rice vinegar, ginger, and garlic.
2. **Marinate the Beef**: Place the beef cubes in a resealable plastic bag or bowl, pour the marinade over, and refrigerate for at least 2 hours or overnight for maximum flavor.
3. **Skewer the Beef**: Thread the marinated beef onto skewers.
4. **Grill**: Preheat a grill or grill pan over medium-high heat. Grill the skewers for 3-4 minutes on each side until cooked to your preferred level of doneness.
5. **Serve**: Garnish with sesame seeds and serve hot.

Miso-Braised Pork Belly

Ingredients:

- 1 lb pork belly, cut into 1-inch cubes
- 3 tbsp white miso paste
- 2 tbsp soy sauce
- 1 tbsp rice vinegar
- 1 tbsp sugar
- 2 cups chicken broth
- 2 cloves garlic, minced
- 1-inch piece of ginger, sliced
- 2 tbsp sesame oil

Instructions:

1. **Sear the Pork Belly**: Heat sesame oil in a large pot over medium-high heat. Brown the pork belly cubes on all sides, then remove and set aside.
2. **Prepare the Braise**: In the same pot, add the garlic, ginger, miso paste, soy sauce, rice vinegar, sugar, and chicken broth. Stir to combine and bring to a simmer.
3. **Braise the Pork Belly**: Return the pork belly to the pot, cover, and simmer on low heat for 1.5 to 2 hours, stirring occasionally, until the pork is tender.
4. **Serve**: Serve the braised pork belly with steamed rice or vegetables.

Miso-Roasted Mushrooms

Ingredients:

- 2 cups mixed mushrooms (shiitake, cremini, or button), sliced
- 2 tbsp white miso paste
- 1 tbsp olive oil
- 1 tbsp soy sauce
- 1 tsp rice vinegar
- 1/2 tsp sesame oil
- 2 cloves garlic, minced
- 1 tbsp fresh parsley, chopped

Instructions:

1. **Preheat the Oven**: Preheat your oven to 400°F (200°C).
2. **Prepare the Mushrooms**: In a large bowl, combine the mushrooms with miso paste, olive oil, soy sauce, rice vinegar, sesame oil, and garlic. Toss to coat.
3. **Roast the Mushrooms**: Spread the mushrooms on a baking sheet in a single layer. Roast for 20-25 minutes, stirring halfway through, until tender and golden.
4. **Serve**: Garnish with fresh parsley and serve as a side dish or topping for rice or noodles.

Miso-Avocado Toast

Ingredients:

- 1 ripe avocado
- 1 tbsp white miso paste
- 2 slices of toasted bread
- 1 tbsp sesame oil
- 1 tsp lemon juice
- 1/2 tsp chili flakes (optional)
- Sesame seeds for garnish

Instructions:

1. **Mash the Avocado**: In a bowl, mash the avocado with miso paste, sesame oil, lemon juice, and chili flakes.
2. **Prepare the Toast**: Spread the miso-avocado mixture on top of toasted bread.
3. **Garnish**: Sprinkle sesame seeds on top and serve immediately as a savory breakfast or snack.

Miso and Green Bean Salad

Ingredients:

- 2 cups green beans, trimmed
- 2 tbsp white miso paste
- 1 tbsp sesame oil
- 1 tbsp rice vinegar
- 1 tsp soy sauce
- 1 tsp honey
- 1/4 cup toasted sesame seeds
- 1/4 cup chopped green onions

Instructions:

1. **Blanch the Green Beans**: Bring a pot of salted water to a boil. Add the green beans and cook for 3-4 minutes until tender-crisp. Drain and immediately transfer to a bowl of ice water to stop the cooking process.
2. **Prepare the Dressing**: In a small bowl, whisk together miso paste, sesame oil, rice vinegar, soy sauce, and honey.
3. **Toss the Salad**: Toss the blanched green beans with the dressing until evenly coated.
4. **Serve**: Garnish with sesame seeds and chopped green onions. Serve chilled or at room temperature.

Miso-Infused Pesto

Ingredients:

- 1 cup fresh basil leaves
- 1/4 cup pine nuts
- 2 tbsp white miso paste
- 1/2 cup olive oil
- 2 cloves garlic
- 1/4 cup grated Parmesan cheese

Instructions:

1. **Blend the Ingredients**: In a food processor, combine basil, pine nuts, miso paste, garlic, and Parmesan cheese.
2. **Add the Olive Oil**: While the processor is running, slowly drizzle in the olive oil until the pesto reaches your desired consistency.
3. **Serve**: Use the pesto with pasta, roasted vegetables, or as a spread.

Miso and Shiitake Mushroom Soup

Ingredients:

- 1 cup dried shiitake mushrooms
- 4 cups vegetable broth
- 2 tbsp white miso paste
- 1 tbsp soy sauce
- 1/2 tsp sesame oil
- 2 green onions, chopped
- 1 block tofu, cubed (optional)

Instructions:

1. **Rehydrate the Mushrooms**: Place the dried shiitake mushrooms in hot water for 20 minutes to rehydrate, then slice thinly.
2. **Make the Soup Base**: In a pot, combine the vegetable broth, miso paste, soy sauce, and sesame oil. Bring to a simmer.
3. **Add the Mushrooms and Tofu**: Add the sliced mushrooms and tofu (if using) to the broth. Simmer for 5-10 minutes.
4. **Serve**: Garnish with chopped green onions and serve hot.

Miso-Maple Roasted Squash

Ingredients:

- 1 medium squash (butternut or acorn), peeled and cubed
- 2 tbsp white miso paste
- 1 tbsp maple syrup
- 1 tbsp olive oil
- 1 tbsp soy sauce
- 1/2 tsp ground cinnamon

Instructions:

1. **Preheat the Oven**: Preheat your oven to 375°F (190°C).
2. **Prepare the Squash**: In a bowl, toss the cubed squash with miso paste, maple syrup, olive oil, soy sauce, and cinnamon.
3. **Roast the Squash**: Spread the squash in a single layer on a baking sheet. Roast for 25-30 minutes, flipping halfway through, until tender and golden.
4. **Serve**: Serve as a side dish or over quinoa for a hearty meal.

Miso Braised Short Ribs

Ingredients:

- 2 lbs beef short ribs
- 3 tbsp white miso paste
- 2 tbsp soy sauce
- 1 tbsp sesame oil
- 1 tbsp rice vinegar
- 3 cups beef broth
- 1-inch piece of ginger, sliced
- 2 cloves garlic, minced

Instructions:

1. **Brown the Short Ribs**: In a large pot, heat sesame oil over medium-high heat. Brown the short ribs on all sides, then remove and set aside.
2. **Prepare the Braise**: In the same pot, add the garlic, ginger, miso paste, soy sauce, rice vinegar, and beef broth. Stir to combine and bring to a simmer.
3. **Braise the Short Ribs**: Return the short ribs to the pot, cover, and simmer for 2-3 hours, until the meat is tender and falls off the bone.
4. **Serve**: Serve the braised short ribs with the braising liquid and mashed potatoes or rice.

Miso and Soba Noodle Salad

Ingredients:

- 8 oz soba noodles
- 2 tbsp white miso paste
- 2 tbsp soy sauce
- 1 tbsp rice vinegar
- 1 tbsp sesame oil
- 1 tsp grated ginger
- 1 carrot, julienned
- 1 cucumber, julienned
- 2 green onions, sliced
- 1 tbsp sesame seeds

Instructions:

1. **Cook the Soba Noodles**: Cook the soba noodles according to package instructions, drain, and rinse under cold water.
2. **Prepare the Dressing**: In a bowl, whisk together miso paste, soy sauce, rice vinegar, sesame oil, and ginger.
3. **Assemble the Salad**: Toss the noodles, carrot, cucumber, and green onions with the dressing.
4. **Serve**: Garnish with sesame seeds and serve chilled or at room temperature.

Miso and Coconut Soup

Ingredients:

- 4 cups vegetable broth
- 1 cup coconut milk
- 2 tbsp white miso paste
- 1 tbsp soy sauce
- 1 tsp grated ginger
- 1/2 cup sliced mushrooms
- 1/2 cup tofu, cubed
- 1/4 cup chopped green onions

Instructions:

1. **Prepare the Broth**: In a pot, combine vegetable broth, coconut milk, miso paste, soy sauce, and ginger. Bring to a simmer.
2. **Add Mushrooms and Tofu**: Stir in the mushrooms and tofu, and cook for 5-7 minutes until tender.
3. **Serve**: Garnish with chopped green onions and serve hot.

Miso-Glazed Tofu Bites

Ingredients:

- 1 block of firm tofu, cut into cubes
- 2 tbsp white miso paste
- 1 tbsp soy sauce
- 1 tbsp maple syrup or honey
- 1 tsp sesame oil
- 1 tsp rice vinegar
- Sesame seeds, for garnish

Instructions:

1. **Prepare the Glaze**: In a bowl, mix miso paste, soy sauce, maple syrup, sesame oil, and rice vinegar.
2. **Marinate the Tofu**: Toss the tofu cubes in the miso glaze and let sit for 15-20 minutes.
3. **Cook the Tofu**: Preheat a skillet over medium heat and cook the tofu for 5-7 minutes on each side until golden brown.
4. **Serve**: Garnish with sesame seeds and serve as a snack or with rice.

Miso and Garlic Sautéed Greens

Ingredients:

- 1 bunch kale or spinach, chopped
- 1 tbsp white miso paste
- 1 clove garlic, minced
- 1 tbsp olive oil
- 1 tbsp soy sauce
- 1 tsp rice vinegar

Instructions:

1. **Prepare the Sauce**: In a small bowl, mix miso paste, soy sauce, and rice vinegar.
2. **Sauté the Garlic and Greens**: Heat olive oil in a skillet over medium heat, add garlic, and cook until fragrant. Add the greens and sauté until wilted.
3. **Add the Sauce**: Stir in the miso sauce and cook for an additional 2 minutes.
4. **Serve**: Serve hot as a side dish.

Miso-Marinated Tempeh

Ingredients:

- 8 oz tempeh, sliced
- 2 tbsp white miso paste
- 1 tbsp soy sauce
- 1 tbsp maple syrup
- 1 tsp sesame oil
- 1/2 tsp rice vinegar

Instructions:

1. **Prepare the Marinade**: In a bowl, whisk together miso paste, soy sauce, maple syrup, sesame oil, and rice vinegar.
2. **Marinate the Tempeh**: Place the tempeh slices in the marinade for at least 30 minutes or overnight.
3. **Cook the Tempeh**: Grill or pan-fry the tempeh for 3-4 minutes per side until golden.
4. **Serve**: Serve as a main dish or sandwich filling.

Miso-Mustard Grilled Chicken

Ingredients:

- 4 chicken thighs or breasts
- 2 tbsp white miso paste
- 1 tbsp Dijon mustard
- 1 tbsp soy sauce
- 1 tbsp honey
- 1 tbsp olive oil

Instructions:

1. **Prepare the Marinade**: In a bowl, combine miso paste, Dijon mustard, soy sauce, honey, and olive oil.
2. **Marinate the Chicken**: Coat the chicken with the marinade and refrigerate for at least 1 hour.
3. **Grill the Chicken**: Grill over medium heat for 6-8 minutes per side, until the chicken is cooked through.
4. **Serve**: Serve hot with a side of vegetables or salad.

Miso and Lemon Grilled Shrimp

Ingredients:

- 1 lb shrimp, peeled and deveined
- 2 tbsp white miso paste
- 1 tbsp lemon juice
- 1 tbsp olive oil
- 1 tsp soy sauce
- 1 tsp grated ginger

Instructions:

1. **Prepare the Marinade**: In a bowl, whisk together miso paste, lemon juice, olive oil, soy sauce, and ginger.
2. **Marinate the Shrimp**: Toss the shrimp in the marinade and let sit for 15-20 minutes.
3. **Grill the Shrimp**: Grill the shrimp for 2-3 minutes per side until pink and opaque.
4. **Serve**: Serve as an appetizer or over rice.

Miso Braised Duck

Ingredients:

- 4 duck legs
- 3 tbsp white miso paste
- 2 tbsp soy sauce
- 1 tbsp rice vinegar
- 1 tbsp honey
- 2 cups chicken broth
- 1-inch piece of ginger, sliced
- 2 cloves garlic, minced

Instructions:

1. **Sear the Duck Legs**: Heat a skillet over medium heat and sear the duck legs skin-side down until golden, then flip and sear the other side.
2. **Prepare the Braise**: In a large pot, combine miso paste, soy sauce, rice vinegar, honey, chicken broth, ginger, and garlic.
3. **Braise the Duck**: Place the duck legs in the pot, cover, and simmer on low heat for 2-3 hours until the duck is tender and falls off the bone.
4. **Serve**: Serve with steamed rice or vegetables, drizzling some of the braising liquid over the duck.

Miso-Infused Creamy Polenta

Ingredients:

- 1 cup polenta
- 4 cups water or vegetable broth
- 1 tbsp white miso paste
- 1/2 cup grated Parmesan cheese
- 2 tbsp butter
- Salt and pepper to taste

Instructions:

1. **Cook the Polenta**: In a saucepan, bring water or broth to a boil. Gradually whisk in the polenta, reduce heat, and simmer, stirring often, until thick and creamy (about 20-25 minutes).
2. **Add Miso and Seasonings**: Stir in the miso paste, Parmesan, butter, salt, and pepper.
3. **Serve**: Serve warm as a side dish or base for vegetables or meat.

Miso and Lime Shrimp Tacos

Ingredients:

- 1 lb shrimp, peeled and deveined
- 2 tbsp white miso paste
- Juice of 1 lime
- 1 tbsp olive oil
- 1 tsp chili powder
- Corn tortillas
- Shredded cabbage, avocado slices, and cilantro for toppings

Instructions:

1. **Marinate the Shrimp**: In a bowl, mix miso paste, lime juice, olive oil, and chili powder. Add the shrimp and marinate for 15 minutes.
2. **Cook the Shrimp**: Heat a skillet over medium heat and cook the shrimp for 2-3 minutes per side until pink and cooked through.
3. **Assemble Tacos**: Warm tortillas, then fill with shrimp, cabbage, avocado, and cilantro.

Spicy Miso Dressing for Salads

Ingredients:

- 2 tbsp white miso paste
- 1 tbsp soy sauce
- 1 tbsp rice vinegar
- 1 tsp sesame oil
- 1 tsp sriracha or chili paste (adjust for spice)
- 1 tsp honey or maple syrup

Instructions:

1. **Mix Ingredients**: In a small bowl, whisk together miso paste, soy sauce, rice vinegar, sesame oil, sriracha, and honey.
2. **Serve**: Drizzle over salads or use as a dressing for roasted vegetables.

Miso-Infused Vegetable Tempura

Ingredients:

- Assorted vegetables (zucchini, sweet potato, bell peppers)
- 1 cup cold water
- 1 cup flour
- 1 tbsp white miso paste
- Oil for frying

Instructions:

1. **Prepare the Batter**: Whisk miso paste into cold water until dissolved. Slowly add flour, stirring until just combined.
2. **Dip and Fry**: Heat oil in a skillet. Dip vegetables into batter and fry until golden and crispy.
3. **Serve**: Serve with dipping sauce of choice.

Miso Pork Ramen

Ingredients:

- 1 lb pork shoulder or belly, sliced
- 4 cups chicken or pork broth
- 2 tbsp white miso paste
- 2 cloves garlic, minced
- 1 tbsp soy sauce
- Ramen noodles, cooked
- Toppings: green onions, boiled egg, nori, corn

Instructions:

1. **Sear the Pork**: In a pot, sear pork slices until browned.
2. **Prepare the Broth**: Add broth, miso paste, garlic, and soy sauce. Simmer for 30 minutes to develop flavor.
3. **Assemble the Ramen**: Add cooked noodles to bowls, pour over the broth, and top with pork and desired toppings.

Miso-Curry Rice

Ingredients:

- 2 cups cooked rice
- 1 tbsp white miso paste
- 1 tsp curry powder
- 1 tbsp soy sauce
- 1/2 cup mixed vegetables (peas, carrots)

Instructions:

1. **Prepare Seasoning**: In a small bowl, mix miso paste, curry powder, and soy sauce.
2. **Combine with Rice**: Toss the cooked rice and vegetables with the seasoning until evenly coated.
3. **Serve**: Serve warm as a side or main dish.

Miso Gravy for Mashed Potatoes

Ingredients:

- 2 tbsp butter
- 2 tbsp flour
- 2 cups vegetable or chicken broth
- 1 tbsp white miso paste
- Salt and pepper to taste
Instructions:
1. **Make the Roux**: In a saucepan, melt butter and add flour, stirring until golden.
2. **Add Broth and Miso**: Gradually whisk in broth and miso paste, simmering until thickened.
3. **Serve**: Serve over mashed potatoes.

Miso and Pumpkin Soup

Ingredients:

- 1 cup pumpkin puree
- 3 cups vegetable broth
- 1 tbsp white miso paste
- 1 tsp grated ginger
- 1/2 cup coconut milk

Instructions:

1. **Combine Ingredients**: In a pot, combine pumpkin puree, broth, miso paste, and ginger. Bring to a simmer.
2. **Add Coconut Milk**: Stir in coconut milk and cook for another 5 minutes.
3. **Serve**: Serve warm, garnished with cilantro or pumpkin seeds.

Miso-Cilantro Rice

Ingredients:

- 2 cups cooked rice
- 1 tbsp white miso paste
- 1/4 cup fresh cilantro, chopped
- 1 tbsp rice vinegar
- 1 tbsp olive oil

Instructions:

1. **Mix Miso Sauce**: In a small bowl, whisk together miso paste, rice vinegar, and olive oil.
2. **Combine with Rice**: Toss cooked rice with miso sauce and cilantro until well combined.
3. **Serve**: Serve as a side dish with grilled fish or chicken.

www.ingramcontent.com/pod-product-compliance
Lightning Source LLC
LaVergne TN
LVHW061950070526
838199LV00060B/4067